3 1842 03044 4911

PIANO • VOCAL • GUITAR

MODERN WORSHIP CHRISTMAS
FOR PIANO

Produced by
Alfred Music
P.O. Box 10003
Van Nuys, CA 91410-0003
alfred.com

Printed in USA.

ISBN-10: 1-4706-2768-X
ISBN-13: 978-1-4706-2768-3

ARTIST INDEX

CONTENTS

ANGELS WE HAVE HEARD ON HIGH

Words and Music by
CHRIS TOMLIN and ED CASH

BORN IS THE KING

(It's Christmas)

Words and Music by
MATT CROCKER and
SCOTT LIGERTWOOD

Moderate rock ♩ = 100

Do do do do do do do do do do do do do. Do do do do do do do

Verse 1:

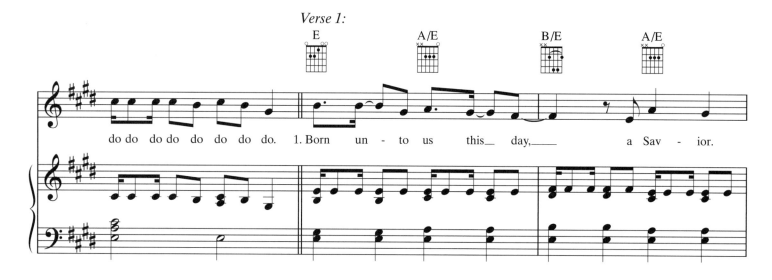

do do do do do do do do. 1. Born un-to us this__ day,__ a Sav-ior.

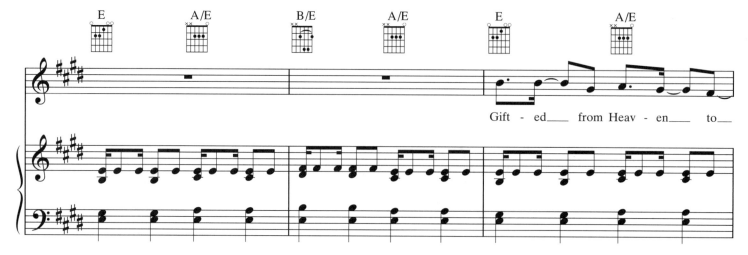

Gift-ed__ from Heav-en__ to__

BORN THAT WE MAY HAVE LIFE

Words and Music by
ED CASH, CHRIS TOMLIN and MATT MAHER

18

19

Born That We May Have Life - 7 - 4

CHRISTMAS OFFERING

Words and Music by
PAUL BALOCHE

*Optional Guitar Capo 1.

Christmas Offering - 5 - 1

EMMANUEL

Words and Music by
MICHAEL W. SMITH

Joyfully ♩ = 126

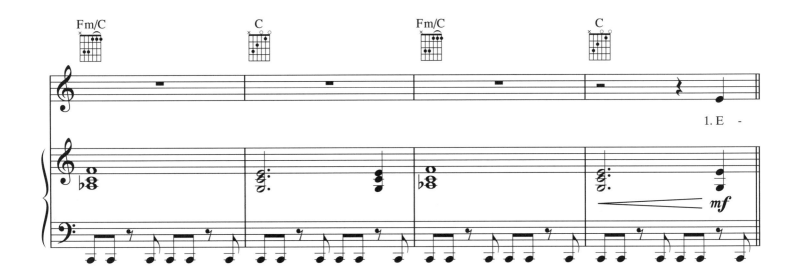

Verses 1 & 2:

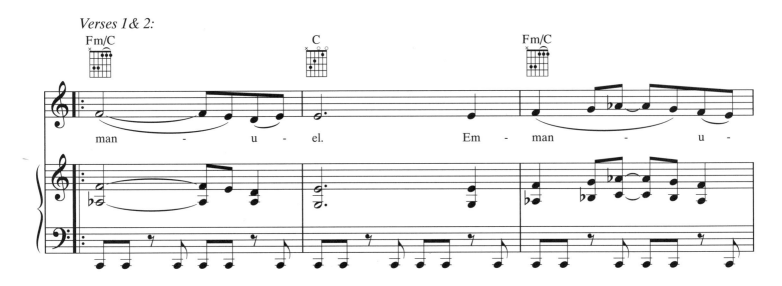

Emmanuel - 5 - 2

EMMANUEL
(Hallowed Manger Ground)

Words and Music by
ED CASH and CHRIS TOMLIN

Gently and reverently ♩. = 48

(with pedal)

Verse 1:

hope we hold___ this star-lit___ night; a King is born___ in Beth-le-hem.___ Our

jour-ney long,___ we seek the light___ that leads to the hal-low-ed man - ger

* Optional Guitar Capo 5.

Emmanuel (Hallowed Manger Ground) - 5 - 1

36

HALLELUJAH

Words and Music by
DARLENE ZSCHECH

Moderately slow ♩ = 70

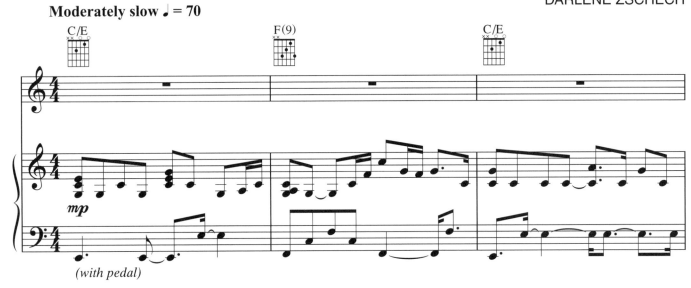

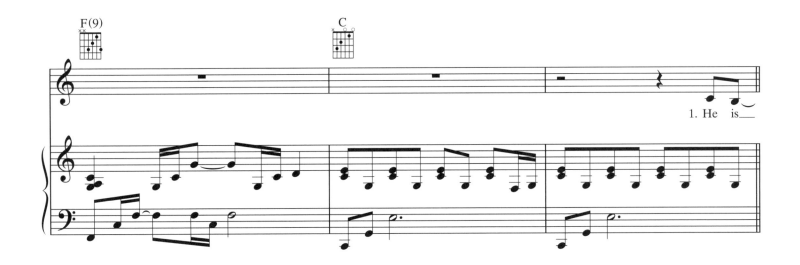

1. He is__

Verse:

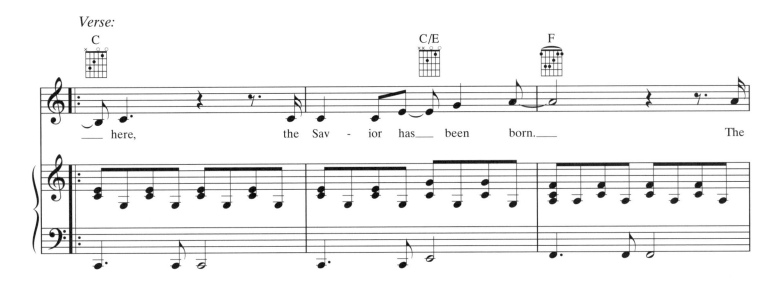

__ here, the Sav - ior has__ been born.__ The

Chorus:

41

42

HALLELUJAH
(Light Has Come)

Words and Music by
BARLOWGIRL

Verse 1:

1. Mmm_____ my Ba - by, heav - en sent You to me. All the world's_ been pray-

44

Hallelujah (Light Has Come) - 7 - 2

Verse 2:

HARK! THE HERALD ANGELS SING/
KING OF HEAVEN

HARK! THE HERALD ANGELS SING
Traditional
Arranged by PAUL BALOCHE

KING OF HEAVEN
Words and Music by
JASON INGRAM and PAUL BALOCHE

Moderate acoustic rock ♩ = 110

Hey!   Hey!

Verses 1 & 2:

1. Hark! The her - ald an - gels sing.___ Glo - ry to the new - born King.
2. Hail, the heav'n - born Prince of Peace.___ Hail the Son of Right - eous - ness.

* Optional Guitar Capo 1.

Hark! The Herald Angels Sing/King of Heaven - 7 - 1

52

56

HE HAS COME FOR US

(God Rest Ye Merry, Gentlemen)

Words and Music by
MEREDITH ANDREWS
and JASON INGRAM

Moderately slow rock (♩ = 66)

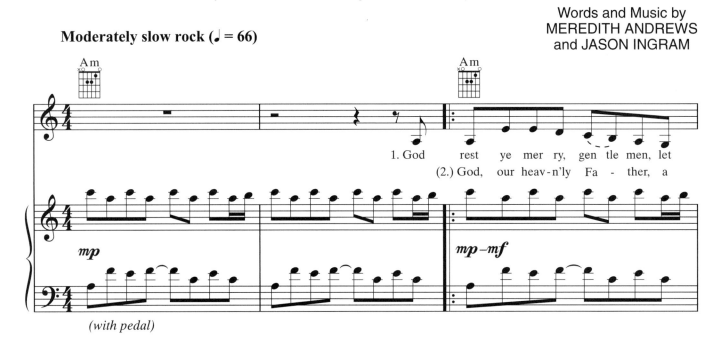

(with pedal)

noth-ing you dis-may. Re-mem-ber Christ, our Sav-ior was born on Christ-mas day to
bless-ed an-gel came. And un-to cer-tain shep-herds brought tid-ings of the same. How

save us all from Sa-tan's pow'r when we were gone a-stray.
that in Beth-le-hem was born the Son of God by name. } O,___ tid-ings of com-fort and

He Has Come for Us (God Rest Ye Merry, Gentlemen) - 4 - 1

HOW MANY KINGS

Words and Music by
MARC MARTEL and
JASON GERMAIN

*Original recording up 1 whole step in B major, guitar capo IV.

64

All for you._____ All for
me._____ All for you._____
All for__ me._____ All for
you._____ All for me._____

I HEARD THE BELLS ON CHRISTMAS DAY

Words and Music by
DALE OLIVER, MARK HALL
and BERNIE HERMS

Moderately slow ♩ = 73

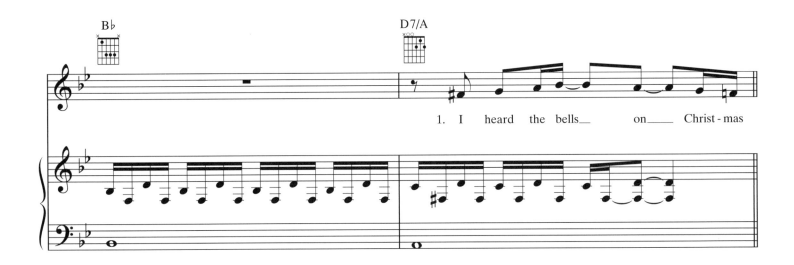

(with pedal)

1. I heard the bells__ on__ Christ - mas

Verses 1 & 2:

Day.
head.

Their old__ fa - mil - liar car - ols
"There is__ no peace on earth," I

73

I Heard the Bells on Christmas Day - 7 - 6

74

JOSEPH'S LULLABY

Words and Music by
BROWN BANNISTER
and BART MILLARD

Joseph's Lullaby - 5 - 1

JESUS MESSIAH

Words and Music by
DANIEL CARSON, CHRIS TOMLIN,
ED CASH and JESSE REEVES

Moderately slow ♩ = 83

*Original recording is in B Major. Optional Capo 4.

Jesus Messiah - 8 - 1

JOY TO THE WORLD (UNSPEAKABLE JOY)

Arrangement and Additional Chorus by
ED CASH, MATT GILDER and CHRIS TOMLIN

90

Chorus:

Chorus:

MY SOUL MAGNIFIES THE LORD

Words and Music by
CHRIS TOMLIN and
DANIEL CARSON

Verse:

1. Good news of great joy for ev'ry wom-an, ev'ry man. This will be a sign to you,
(2.) com-pa-ny of an - gels, "Glo-ry in the high - est!" And on the earth, a peace a-mong
3. Un - to you a Child is born, un - to us, a Son is giv'n. Let ev - 'ry heart pre-pare His throne,

Bridge:

My Soul Magnifies the Lord - 9 - 9

O HOLY NIGHT

Words and Music by
CHRIS TOMLIN

*Optional Guitar Capo 5 in G major.

O Holy Night - 7 - 1

D.S. % al Coda

O Holy Night - 7 - 5

WHAT CAN I DO
(Christmas Version)

Words and Music by
GRAHAM KENDRICK
and PAUL BALOCHE

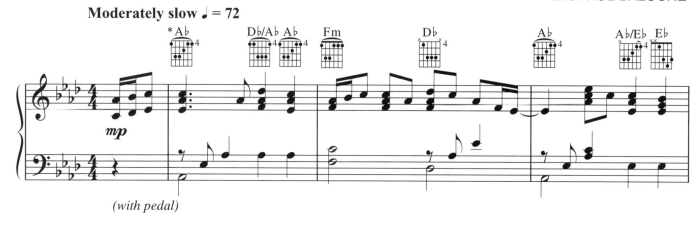

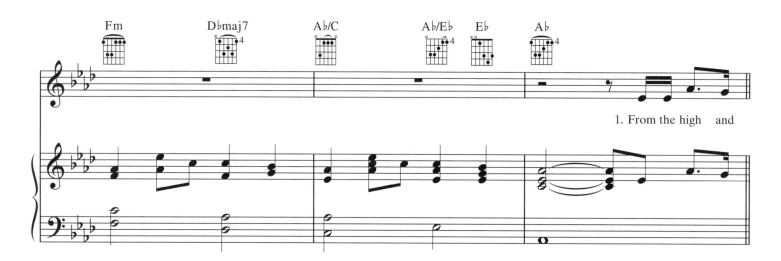

1. From the high and

Verse:

ho - ly to a man-ger low - ly, the great-est mys-ter-y the world has ev - er
low - est You be-came as one of us. In our grief and bro-ken-ness You suf-fered by___ our

*Optional Guitar Capo 1 in G.

116

YOUR NAME
(Christmas Version)

Words and Music by
GLENN PACKIAM and PAUL BALOCHE

*Optional Capo 3 in G major

Your Name (Christmas Version) - 6 - 1

na - tions sing it loud - er, 'cause noth - ing has___ the pow - er to save___

but Your Name.___

but Your Name.___

Bridge:

cresc.

WHEN HOPE CAME DOWN

Words and Music by
BEN GLOVER
and KARI JOBE

Moderately ♩ = 100

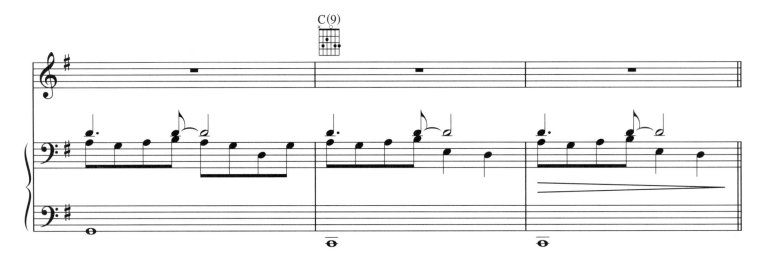

Verse:

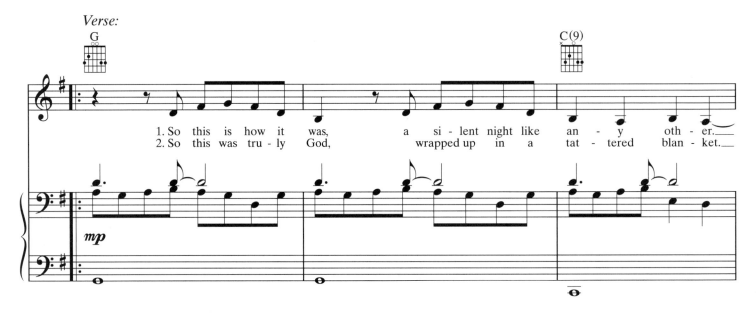

1. So this is how it was, a si - lent night like an - y oth - er.
2. So this was tru - ly God, wrapped up in a tat - tered blan - ket.

When Hope Came Down - 5 - 1